The UNBELIEVABLE CRYPTOZOOLOGY

COLORING BOOK

George Toufexis

Dover Publications, Inc.
Mineola, New York

In this fascinating coloring book you can explore the mysterious world of cryptozoology! Cryptozoology means the study of hidden animals and within the pages of this book you will find thirty legendary creatures who may or may not exist. Along with such famous cryptids (creatures whose existence has not been scientifically proven) as Bigfoot and the Loch Ness Monster, you will find the terrifying Chupacabra, the infamous Lizard Man of South Carolina, and the fierce Emela-Ntouka of Central Africa. So get your crayons, markers, and colored pencils ready as you venture into the realm of cryptozoology.

Bibliographical Note
The Unbelievable Cryptozoology Coloring Book is a new work, first published by Dover Publications, Inc., in 2012.

International Standard Book Number
ISBN-13: 978-0-486-78053-5
ISBN-10: 0-486-78053-8

Manufactured in the United States by LSC Communications
78053803   2017
www.doverpublications.com

CRYPTOZOOLOGY

There is a class of creatures that seem to exist on our planet—hidden in the dark forests, out in desolate wilderness places and in the ocean deep. They are called cryptids (from the greek word "crypto" which means "hidden") and they exist outside the standard world of science. Are they real? There is no conclusive evidence, but it's fun to imagine what they look like. All the creatures depicted in this book are based on eyewitness testimony.

THE LOCH NESS MONSTER

This legendary creature inhabits one of the largest freshwater lakes in the country of Scotland, which
has become famous for sightings of this mysterious monster. The earliest "Nessie" sighting comes from
a man named Adamnan who wrote over 1,200 years ago, during the Dark Ages. He describes how in
565 A.D. the famous monk Columba saved someone who was being attacked by a fierce lake monster!

THE CHUPACABRA
Most sightings of this strange creature come from the Southwestern USA and Mexico, as well as Florida and Puerto Rico, but reports have come from as far north as Maine and as far south as Chile. The name actually means "goat sucker," which seems to be their dinner of choice.

BIGFOOT (Sasquatch)
Probably the most famous and most sought after cryptid in recent history. Reports of sightings have come from all over the USA and Canada concerning this large, hairy, ape-like humanoid.

FANGOLOBOLO
This creature roams the night skies over the dark jungles of the island of Madagascar off the east coast of southern Africa. Described as giant vampire bats with a ten foot wing span, it has been alleged to attack humans.

ARICA MONSTER
A reptilian creature seen in the desert region of Chile in South America.
On desert roads, people have reported seeing a strange beast with leathery
skin and razor-sharp teeth running at high speed on it's hind legs,
similar to a raptor.

THE YETI

High up in the Himalaya mountains of Asia there lurks an ape-like entity known and feared by local people and climbers. This large creature is called Yeti, (rock bear) Michay, (man-bear) or Migoi, which means "wild man." In the early part of the 20th century it became known as "The Abominable Snowman."

MAMLAMBO
*Newspapers recently reported sightings of a "giant reptile" monster
in the Mzintlava River in South Africa that had supposedly killed several people.
It was claimed that the monster was over 60 feet long, had the head of a horse, body of a
fish, neck of a snake, and that it glowed green at night.*

THE LIZARD MAN
The Lizard Man of Lee County, South Carolina, is said to be 7 feet tall, muscular, and covered in dark, scaly reptilian skin. Eyewitnesses claim that the creature is incredibly strong and can easily rip a car apart. Some experts suggest that the Lizard Man is the result of mutation due to toxic chemicals.

The LUSCA
The waters of the Bahamas off the east coast of Florida have a creature that has terrorized fishermen and divers for years. It is a giant octopus known as the Lusca. It usually hides in caves and crevices in the deeper waters and in strange areas known as "Blue Holes," but has been known to attack boats along the surface.

MNGWA

Peoples of eastern Africa describe an animal that they insist is not a lion or any other of the known big cats. They call it the Mngwa. It is described as being larger than a leopard (the size of a donkey), with grayish fur, large teeth and claws and a ferocious nature. Some speculate that it is a previously unknown type of tiger.

OGOPOGO
Ogopogo (lake demon) is a lake monster said to live in Lake Okanagan, B.C., Canada. This many-humped creature has been seen for ages by the native people and reported by settlers since the 19th century. It's described as having a large head and is estimated to be 40 to 50-feet-long. Experts have suggested it may be a kind of primitive whale such as a Basilosaurus.

THE BEAST OF BUSCO
In 1898, a farmer claimed he saw a giant turtle living in the lake on his farm near Churubusco.
In 1948, 2 more people reported seeing a huge turtle (500 pounds) while fishing on the same lake.
Large groups of sightseers arrived and the search began. Police, hunters, scientists and reporters
tried to find proof, but the beast has eluded them so far.

THE KONGAMATO
People of Zambia and other areas of Africa have claimed to see a large creature with leathery wings and a sharp beak. The name Kongamato translated means "breaker of boats." This bad-tempered creature has allegedly attacked people on several occasions.

CHUCHUNYA

This is a man-like creature rumoured to exist in the remote forests of Siberia in Russia. It has been described as seven feet tall and covered with dark hair. Some experts have speculated that Chuchunya may be a long lost group of Neanderthals, a form of prehistoric human.

PHAYA NAGA
This creature supposedly inhabits the Mekong River in Cambodia and Thailand. It has a body like a python and the head of a dragon, and images of the beast are found in many temples throughout the region.

THE JERSEY DEVIL
This is a creature that has been seen in the dark forests of Southern New Jersey, USA. It is usually described as having 2 legs with hooves, a goat-like head with horns, arms with clawed hands and leathery wings on it's back. Witnesses claim it is very quick and often sends out a blood-curdling scream!

VAN LAKE MONSTER

First reported by a Turkish newspaper in 1889 that a large creature dragged a man into Lake Van, a large lake in Eastern Turkey, there have now been more than 1,000 people who claim to have seen the beast which measures over 50 feet long. It is said to have spikes on its back and appears similar to a Plesiosaur or other aquatic dinosaur.

GIANT LAKE WORM

Lagarfljót is a lake in a remote region of Iceland where from 1345 to the present, people have been seeing a gigantic worm. This creature is often sighted raising its back above the the cold, dark glacier water of the lake. It is described as longer than a football field, (300 feet), and has also been seen outside the water, lying coiled up or slithering into the trees.

DINGONEK

Living around the rivers and lakes of western Africa, the Dingonek is roughly 12-feet in length, with a large horn on its head, long canine teeth (giving it the nickname "Jungle Walrus") and a tail that is supposed to be poisonous. It is said to be covered in a scaly skin like the Asian anteater known as the pangolin.

THE MOTHMAN
On a cold night in 1966, gravediggers in West Virginia claimed to have seen a man-like figure fly low from the trees over their heads. A few days later, two young couples told police they saw a large creature with ten-foot wings whose eyes glowed red. More sightings followed and that was the beginning of the Mothman legend.

MOKELE-MBEMBE
This is a large reptilian creature, with a long neck and long tail. Even though it eats plants it is said to roar loudly if approached by humans. So far, there have been more than 50 expeditions to the remote jungles of the Congo in Africa but no evidence, except for the large claw-shaped footprint found by a French missionary in 1776.

PINATUBO MONSTERS
Mount Pinatubo, a volcano in the Phillipines, erupted in recent times and after a while, disturbing reprorts of villagers being attacked by packs of creatures that were a cross between an eel and a shark were received by authorites. Did the volcano have anything to do with releasing these beasts into the water?

THE ROPEN

The Ropen is a flying creature that glows briefly as it flies over the remote jungles of Papua New Guinea in southeast Asia. It is said to feed on fish, but there are some reports of Ropen attacking humans. It has leather wings and a small body, thus many people believe it to be a surviving Pterosaur, thought to be long extinct.

EMELA-NTOUKA

This animal is about the size of a large rhinoceros, and like a rhino, has a long horn on its snout. It lives in the swamps and lakes of the Congo River basin in Central Africa. The natives of the area rightly treat this creature with great fear.

MONGOLIAN DEATH WORMS
A creature reported to exist in the Gobi Desert of east central Asia. It is a bright red worm with a wide body that is 2 to 5 feet long. Mongolian natives claim the worm can spit burning acid that can kill a human. They also say that the worms kill at a distance using electricity.

THE BEAR LAKE MONSTER
This creature gets its name from sightings near Bear Lake, in the Utah–Idaho area of the USA. The general description is that it is a serpent with legs (like an alligator) that hunts along the edge of the water. It is about 30 to 50 feet long and can move swiftly through the lake—faster than a horse could run on dry land.

THE BUNYIP
This is a large creature lurking in creeks, riverbeds, and waterholes in Australian swamp and marshes. The word bunyip means "devil" or "evil spirit." Fossilized bones were discovered ne areas of sightings. They were identified as bones of a prehistoric mammal known as Diprotodon.

MEGALODON

Although the giant prehistoric shark known as Megalodon (meaning "large tooth") is believed to have gone extinct ages ago, evidence of its existence in the black depths of the oceans still persist. After all, the idea of a giant squid called "the Kraken" was thought to be a fantasy—until an 80 foot long squid washed ashore on a Danish beach!

GIANT ANACONDA
It is not uncommon to find Anacondas that are over 20 feet long. These huge snakes are feared for good reason. There are many claims of Anacondas that grow to 100 feet long and can swallow a human being in one gulp!